Dr. Grace LaJoy Henderson

Revised Edition

A GIFTED CHILD IN FOSTER CARE

A Story of Resilience

Inspirations by Grace LaJoy
Raymore, MO
www.gracelajoy.com
poetry@gracelajoy.com

A Gifted Child
IN FOSTER CARE

Dr. Grace LaJoy Henderson

Disclaimer.
Due to finding my mother alive after forty-nine years, I have revised A Gifted Child in Foster Care from the original version. My mother and siblings' names are removed or fictitious. Even though I found my mother under an entirely different name, I still removed the original name in this Revised Edition. I made no major revisions to the details of my own recollection of my real-life foster care story.

With the publication of this Revised Edition, the original version has been taken off the market.

A GIFTED CHILD IN FOSTER CARE – REVISED EDITION
Copyright ©2009, Revised 2020. Grace LaJoy Henderson
Published by Inspirations by Grace LaJoy
Raymore, MO
www.gracelajoy.com

Library of Congress Control Number:

ISBN 978-1-7341868-0-2

All rights reserved. No portion of this book may be copied, reproduced or transmitted in any form without prior written permission from the publisher.

Printed in the United States of America

A Gifted Child   *Dr. Grace LaJoy Henderson*
IN FOSTER CARE

More praise for
A GIFTED CHILD IN FOSTER CARE

"**A Gifted Child in Foster Care** is well written, inspiring, and has a beautiful message. It will encourage students in Gifted and Talented Programs to use their gifts."

~**Dr. Grace Ann Ancona**, Coordinator
Gifted and Talented Program
Kansas City Missouri School District

"This book paints a good picture of the basic needs of all children. It lets older youth know they can become someone."

~**Traci Wallin**, MSW,
Foster Care Program Manager
Catholic Charities – Kansas City

"A compelling story and great principles about working with children in foster care. Anyone who reads this will gain a better understanding of how to nurture and build children's lives toward success."

~**Mark Littleton, Th.M.,** Author
Big Bad God of the Bible

"Grace LaJoy's story is proof that when placed in a positive environment, including foster care, children can discover their potential. This book will benefit young adults in foster care and foster parents who have become frustrated with 'the system'. Readers will gain a greater understanding of foster care and what happens from a child's perspective."

~**Ann Graves**, Family Development Specialist
Catholic Charities Family Advocates

Continued →

A Gifted Child
IN FOSTER CARE
                                    Dr. Grace LaJoy Henderson

More praise continued...

"An excellent resource! A powerful tool that will motivate both youth and adults to focus on their dream and achieve their goal."

~**PJ Hill**, Foster Parent
Blue Springs

"...despite obstacles, a child persevered. This book will help educators identify strengths of all students and build upon them."

~**Shanel Watson**, Special Educator
Grandview School District

"Dr. Grace LaJoy's life story is very motivational. ...very powerful and uplifting not only to students, but educators as well."

~**Patricia L. Davis**, Gifted Educator
Superintendent's Scholars Academy

"Overcoming adversity, a woman still excelled! This story reminds me that there are families and children who go through these experiences."

~**Enjoli Sims**, Educator
Lee's Summit School District

A Gifted Child
IN FOSTER CARE

Dr. Grace LaJoy Henderson

Dedication

My mother, who left our family when I was two years old, never to return.

My father, who tried to keep his children together. He passed away in 1990.

My foster parents, who offered me a stable home environment for three years.

My children Aric and Arica

My siblings

Acknowledgments

Sugar Lee Lewis, who encouraged me to write my foster care story.

Educators who noticed my gifts and creative talent, made me aware of it, and helped cultivate it.

A Gifted Child in Foster Care

Dr. Grace LaJoy Henderson

A Gifted Child
IN FOSTER CARE

Dr. Grace LaJoy Henderson

Table of Contents

FOREWORD – DR. SUGAR LEE LEWIS		VIII
FOREWORD – TOM KIRCHER		IX
FOREWORD – PEARLIE MAE WIGGINS		X
INTRODUCTION		1
A WORD FROM THE AUTHOR		3
CHAPTER 1	LEFT BY MOTHER	7
CHAPTER 2	LIVING WITH DADDY	15
CHAPTER 3	GRANDMOTHER	19
CHAPTER 4	LEFT BY FATHER	25
CHAPTER 5	LIVING IN FOSTER CARE	29
CHAPTER 6	SEPARATED FROM SIBLINGS	37
CHAPTER 7	A TYPICAL DAY IN FOSTER CARE	43
CHAPTER 8	HOW FOSTER CARE SHAPED MY LIFE	49
CHAPTER 9	LIFE AFTER FOSTER CARE	53
CHAPTER 10	DADDY LEFT AGAIN	59
CHAPTER 11	PREGNANT AT SEVENTEEN	67
CHAPTER 12	MY GIFT REVEALED	75
CHAPTER 13	EMPOWERMENT FOR YOUTH	79
CHAPTER 14	EMPOWERMENT FOR PARENTS	83
POEM – "HE'S WORTH IT"		86
DISCUSSION TOPICS		88
GRACE LAJOY'S LIFE TIMELINE		93
GLOSSARY OF TERMS		96
INDEX		99
FINDING MOTHER SERIES		101

A Gifted Child
IN FOSTER CARE

Dr. Grace LaJoy Henderson

Foreword

As a gifted and talented educator for fourteen years, I discovered it was uncommon for foster children to be identified as gifted. So, when Dr. Grace LaJoy told me her story of being placed in the gifted and talented program while living in foster care, I was shocked. I could not imagine how she lived in a foster home and came out as successful as she is.

Her story will help many people, motivating at-risk and foster children to discover their gifts. It will help gifted children see how to use their talents and begin to move to the next level. It will give educators insight into the experiences of a gifted child living in foster care, which will in turn guide them in assisting children from various backgrounds. Expanding their knowledge of exceptional education, through enabling them to identify gifted children who have been labeled as at-risk, or who are minorities, will go a long way to correcting this problem.

A Gifted Child in Foster Care will change the way we look at foster children and open the door for the overlooked gifted child. It is a vital resource, which should be read by students and educators; it should be a *requirement* for anyone working with children in foster care. This book will alert us to the fact that foster children are often misunderstood and help us reconsider before we pre-judge children.

If more public school educators work to expose the gifts that lie in students who are exhibiting behavior problems, the dropout rate will diminish and attendance will increase.

~**Dr. Sugar Lee Lewis**, Administrator
Kansas City Missouri School District

A Gifted Child
IN FOSTER CARE

Dr. Grace LaJoy Henderson

Foreword

Dr. Grace LaJoy has penned a touching and well-written chronicle of her childhood within a loving family that had to contend with poverty, mental illness, abandon- ment and other daunting challenges. No matter how tough things got, or the hurdles she faced, this strong and sensitive young woman never wavered in her drive to be successful.

Her trail blazing approach and single-minded struggle to achieve are a model for *all* children coming from diffi- cult circumstances, not just the gifted. Her touching acknowledgement of the role of "Big mama," her foster mother, in her eventual success is a testament to all those foster parents who work tirelessly to change the world 'one child at a time.'

A Gifted Child in Foster Care instills values and encourages hard work and persistence, while addressing the great life challenges faced by children growing up in foster care. It is a great read for foster children, foster parents, caseworkers, CASA volunteers, and juvenile court judges.

~**Tom Kircher**
Director of Illinois Recruitment
Foster and Adoptive Care Coalition

A Gifted Child
IN FOSTER CARE

Dr. Grace LaJoy Henderson

Foreword

While little Grace LaJoy lived in my foster home, I never would have *dreamed* that this young child, who often misbehaved, would one day write a book. As I read **A Gifted Child in Foster Care**, parts of it made me feel ashamed of myself, but other parts caused me to feel extremely proud. She wrote about the high and low points during her three year stay in my home.

As a foster parent for 25 years, I have cared for over 200 youth. I made some mistakes and there were times when my efforts seemed useless. But, my trials and errors taught me the importance of never giving up children. My foster parent trainer, Mrs. Woodstock, told us, "Don't call them *foster* children". She believed children in foster care should be treated as our own. Even though their stay in our home would be temporary, we should love them as if it would be forever.

This book embodies a valuable lesson and great insight for foster parents. Each child who enters foster care will grow up one day. Our job is to treat them with respect while preparing them to go out into the world and be productive human beings. A child's future should not be judged by their negative past experiences, nor should their total character be judged by just one act of disobedience. Each one should be treated as though a special gift lies inside of them, because it does. I feel extremely grateful that "Papa" and I played a part in cultivating the gift inside of Dr. Grace LaJoy.

~**Pearlie Mae "Big Mama" Wiggins**
Dr. Grace LaJoy's foster mother
Kansas City, Missouri

A Gifted Child
IN FOSTER CARE

Dr. Grace LaJoy Henderson

Introduction

Over the years the words "foster child" and "foster care" often breed negative connotations. Children in foster care are often looked upon as not capable of succeeding in life. Children often leave foster care feeling mistreated or abused. **A Gifted Child in Foster Care** leaves the reader with a different, positive definition of "foster child" and "foster care."

In this book, Dr. Grace LaJoy shares her life story of being deserted by her mother, living in foster care, and ending up in a gifted and talented class while still in foster care. She recalls her life story before, during and after foster care. Her turbulent life experiences reveal how she became strong and began to encourage, inspire and empower others through her gift of writing.

Finally, she offers words of inspiration, encouragement, and empowerment to both children and parents. Children learn that they can succeed and impact the lives of others even in the face of adversity. Parents learn specific steps to help children recognize and utilize their gift(s).

A Gifted Child   *Dr. Grace LaJoy Henderson*
IN FOSTER CARE

A Gifted Child in Foster Care was developed as an educational tool to be used with foster care training. It specifically touches on the issues that are prevalent in foster care, making it a perfect resource for children service workers, foster parents and foster children.

Social Service professionals have compared this book to Dave Pelzer's book entitled, *A Child Called "It",* which focuses on child abuse and overcoming adversity. **A Gifted Child in Foster Care** by Grace LaJoy is similar to Pelzer's books because both authors talk about the unfortunate events that caused them to be separated from their parents, their experiences while in foster care, and how they developed the determination to succeed.

A Gifted Child in Foster Care is an amazing story of resilience, proving that even in the midst of difficulties, it is possible to rise above circumstances, work hard and achieve goals.

Introduction   2

A Gifted Child
IN FOSTER CARE

Dr. Grace LaJoy Henderson

A Word from the Author

Two state programs played a major role in shaping me into the person that I have become: The Foster Care Program and the Gifted and Talented Program.

The Foster Care program is a State funded program overseen by the Department of Social Services. When I was in foster care, it provided temporary, short-term or long-term shelter for children who were separated from their natural parents due to circumstances such as abandonment, incarceration, drug use, child abuse, mental or emotional instability, and/or behavior problems. Sometimes foster care became necessary due to problems with the parent, but just as often it became necessary because of behavior issues with the child.

Today, the Foster Care program is different. While it still provides shelter to children who are separated from their natural parent due to the above-named issues, federal laws now prohibit long-term foster care as a goal for children. Under the Adoption and Safe Families Act of 1997, if any child is in foster care for fifteen of any twenty-two-month period, the child's case worker must make a referral to terminate the parental rights of the natural parents. This does not necessarily mean the parent's rights will be

A Gifted Child   *Dr. Grace LaJoy Henderson*
IN FOSTER CARE

terminated by the courts; just that the courts must consider permanency for the child.

Whereas, it used to be that foster care could become necessary because of behavior issues with the child, now Missouri has enacted a Voluntary Placement Act which allows parents to get help through treatment for their child without relinquishing custody.

In addition to shelter, the Foster Care program provides funds for needs such as food, clothing, health, wellness, and counseling for the children. Thus, when a child is placed in foster care, a case worker is assigned to that child. The case worker must ensure that every need of the child is met.

The Gifted and Talented Program is a State funded program overseen by the Department of Education. It is designed to coordinate with school administrators, educators, and parents to provide special education techniques for students who appear to learn faster than other students on their grade level. This program removes "gifted and talented" students from their regular classroom, either temporarily or permanently, and provides them with a wider array of learning experiences.

A Gifted Child   Dr. Grace LaJoy Henderson
IN FOSTER CARE

The learning style used in gifted and talented classes is different from that used in of the regular classroom settings.

The two programs named above helped shape me during my early years when my parents couldn't care for me. The influence of those programs has stayed with me throughout my life.

A Gifted Child
IN FOSTER CARE

Dr. Grace LaJoy Henderson

A Word from the Author   6

A Gifted Child
IN FOSTER CARE

Dr. Grace LaJoy Henderson

1 - *Left by Mother*

For many people who have a loving mother, it's hard to imagine her deserting her child, but that's exactly what happened to me. My mother left when I was two years old and never came back.

I was born weighing eight pounds and fourteen ounces in Kalamazoo, Michigan, a small town just outside of Grand Rapids. According to my birth records, my father took me home from the

"Your mother left, she doesn't want you."

hospital because my mother was unable to be at home due to an extended illness. I was the last of six children that my father and mother birthed together. As the baby of the family, my siblings called me "Gracie."

At the age of two, I was told, "Your mother left, she doesn't want you." My grandmother, who passed away in 1991, fondly remembers my cute, innocent, yet strong reply, "Well, if she don't want me, I don't want her needer!" Because of that reply, my grandmother believed I was a strong, resilient child who would not be deeply affected by this tragedy.

Boy was she wrong! Those unbelievable words, "your mother doesn't want you," devastated me! My cute, innocent reply was my way of "laughing to keep from crying." And that is exactly how I went through life… laughing to keep from crying. My mother's leaving left me with feelings of fear, insecurity and rejection. "If my own mother didn't want me, then who else would want me?" I often thought.

As I grew older, my school mates asked me, "Where is your mother?" I answered, "I don't have a mother." When they inquired further, I replied, "None of your business!" Questions about my mother re-minded me of those turbulent days when I was told she didn't want me. The thought embarrassed me and I did not want my friends at school to know anything about it. Yet, even with the embarrassment I endured, I never blamed her for leaving.

> *"Though I was only two when my mother left, I still remember many things about her,…"*

Though I was only two when my mother left, I still remember many things about her, both good and bad. For example, my mother often walked around the house singing Christian songs, like, "Jesus Loves the Little Children", "This Little Light of Mine", and "Love Lifted Me." I loved that about my mother and I longed to be just like her!

I recall sitting in church beside my father, looking up, and seeing my mother playing the piano on the stage. I wanted so badly to run up there and be with her. I hoped to play the

A Gifted Child
IN FOSTER CARE

Dr. Grace LaJoy Henderson

piano, too! One day when I was in the church day-care center, my mother came in to take me home. Before we left, she proudly showcased how smart I was to the daycare workers. She asked me, "Where is God?" When I pointed my finger up to the sky, she hugged and told me she was very proud of me. That made me feel terrifically smart...like I was her special little girl.

During the day, I stayed with my mother at home while my father worked and my brothers and sisters attended school. I watched as she cleaned up the house. I wanted to do everything she did. One day she sprayed wood cleaner on one of the tables in the living room, gave me a dusting towel, and let me wipe the dust off the table. My mother told me, "Great job. I'm proud of you." Her compliments made me feel like I was a great housekeeper...just like her!

When I was not helping my mother clean up the house, I would go to my parents' room, slip into my mother's closet, and dress up in her clothes and shoes. Those moments were the most fun I remember having while my mother was still with us. Wearing her clothes and shoes made me feel like I was just like her.

There were a couple of not-so-pleasant moments also. My mother, a sweet and giving person, made some homemade cookies one evening for my siblings, the neighborhood children and me. The cookies smelled good and I wanted

Left by Mother

A Gifted Child
IN FOSTER CARE

Dr. Grace LaJoy Henderson

some very badly, but my mother said I needed a bath before I could have some. Naturally, I wanted the cookies immediately, and acted upset that I had to wait until after my bath. I was also afraid the cookies would be gone by the time my bath was over.

As my mother gave me the bath, my siblings and the neighborhood children ate up the cookies. Finally, my bath was over; I went downstairs to the kitchen only to find the plate empty! I was *very* upset. My sisters and brothers felt sorry for me. "Poor Gracie" I heard one of them say. "We didn't save Gracie any cookies." Although *nothing* could replace my mother's homemade cookies, the fact that they seemed genuinely concerned about it made me feel better.

Another not-so-pleasant memory occurred while I was sitting outside on our porch happily eating a cup of popcorn my mother had popped for me. As I sat out there enjoying my popcorn, a three-year-old boy who lived down the street walked over and asked if he could have some. I didn't trust him and refused, but my sweet and giving mother came outside and ordered me to share with the little boy. I did not believe that was a good idea, but I trusted my mother, so I hesitantly gave him my cup of popcorn.

He put my cup up to his mouth as if to drink the popcorn. In my fear of never getting it back, I grabbed the cup back from him. He held it tighter and said, "This is my beer," her. At that time, I didn't understand why she did those things, but I knew she was hurting terribly.

I often wonder what type of life my mother is living today...Is she in a mental institution? Is she happily remarried with a new family? I have tried to find her often, and at the

"I curled up beside her and cried with her"

beginning, I had high hopes. But in the end, I felt great disappointment after spending much time and money only to discover she remained lost. At other times I have felt hurt and rejected because *she* never seemed to try to find *me*.

Overall, I feel a strong sense of love and loyalty towards the beautiful lady who gave me life. I know in my heart I have gained a greater appreciation for life because of her, both for the happy memories, and because she left me to my own resources that resulted in me becoming a resilient adult.

A Gifted Child
IN FOSTER CARE

Dr. Grace LaJoy Henderson

Living with Daddy

A Gifted Child
IN FOSTER CARE

Dr. Grace LaJoy Henderson

2 - *Living with Daddy*

When my mother disappeared, never to return, she left me and my siblings with our father. He acted angry about my mother leaving. "She never did anything for you all" he often said with disappointment. "But, if you all ever want to try to find her, I will take you to look for her." (There was evidence that my mother moved to another state after she left us.)

> *"...my father did all he could to care for us and keep us together."*

Although Daddy abused my mother, he never struck us. While some family members believe my mother left because of her mental illness, I have always believed she left because of his abuse. However, after she left, Daddy faithfully committed his life to raising us as a single father when I was two years old until I turned seven. During that time, my father did all he could to care for us and keep us together.

He woke up early every morning so he could be present at the union by six. He did cement work, and the union sent him out on jobs. He had to arrive by six to ensure that he would get a job pouring concrete sidewalks, steps, and driveways.

Daddy got paid every Friday, so on Friday's he went to the grocery store and brought home bags of food for the

A Gifted Child
IN FOSTER CARE   *Dr. Grace LaJoy Henderson*

family. He also brought home "commodity food" which was given away by the state to assist needy families. It included powdered milk, cheese, and peanut butter. On payday, Daddy also gave us an allowance. He gave my older siblings ten cents and me five cents. Back then, a nickel could buy a lot because stores sold "penny candy." Today, one piece of "penny candy" costs at least ten cents!

When Daddy was home from work, he watched television, listened to music, and sent us to the neighborhood store. He usually lied on the couch while watching his favorite comedy and game shows. Back then, we listened to records, albums, and eight-track tapes, which played our brands of music. Daddy had them all! He enjoyed the blues, love songs, and gospel music. He often listened to eight-track tapes in the car as he drove around the city.

Daddy often gave us money to shop for him at the store. We bought his favorites; cigarettes, a soda pop, and a chocolate candy bar. He also gave us money to buy something we wanted or just let us keep the change.

While living with Daddy, I learned the important concept of "never giving up on your goal." One day, as Daddy sat in the living room watching television, I tried to hurry past him with a slice of cake in my hand. I planned to take the cake *outside* and eat it, even though he told me to eat the cake at the *dining room table*. I was determined to eat the cake outside.

Living with Daddy   16

A Gifted Child
IN FOSTER CARE   *Dr. Grace LaJoy Henderson*

When Daddy wasn't looking, I put the cake inside my shoe and hurried past him, towards the front door. "Did you finish eating your cake?" he asked. I said, "Yes," and he believed me.

When I got outside, I pulled the cake out of my shoe and ate it! This was clearly disobedience, but it also shows how determined I could be about a goal. I'm not sure how sanitary the cake was after all the trouble I went through just to get it outside, but the flavor remained in it when I took it out of my shoe. Was it smashed? Yes, it was. Did it stink? It probably did. But I set a goal, and achieved it.

Overall, Daddy was patient when it came to his children. One evening while he was not home, my siblings and I each made a "dummy" out of old clothes. When we heard him pull into the driveway in his car, we set the dummies on the couch and chairs in the living room and we all hid so that he would think the dummies were us!

When Daddy walked in through the door, he began fussing at the dummies, whipping them with his belt, and telling them to get up and get their housework done! As I kneeled on my knees in my hiding place in the kitchen, I was overtaken with laughter thinking, "we tricked Daddy!"

Looking back on that event, I realize that my daddy knew those dummies were not his children; he was just playing along with us. Although my father did the best he

Living with Daddy   17

A Gifted Child
IN FOSTER CARE

Dr. Grace LaJoy Henderson

could for us, he needed help raising six children. Much of that help came from my grandmother.

3 – *Grandmother*

Grandmother adopted my mother when she was two years old and changed her name, although her mother had given her another name. Grandmother was actually married to my mother's great uncle, whom I never met. That connection led to the adoption.

My mother's real mother had seven children and she had a mental illness, too. She was unable to take care of my mother, who was her youngest child, so she let Grandmother have her. Grandmother told me that, during childhood, Mother was smart and a great pianist.

After my mother disappeared, Grandmother wondered a lot about where she went and why she never came back. Daddy often took me and my two sisters over her house on Saturday mornings so she could wash and press our hair. While there, she let us help make delicious pineapple drop cookies and take leftovers home. She became the beloved "mother" of our family for many years after that.

Grandmother was a great cook and kept her home very neat and clean. We often visited her home for dinner. She also brought homemade food from her freezer to us to help Daddy with meals.

Grandmother introduced me to many things I would otherwise not have experienced. She took me with her when she went to out of town by airplane, to see her favorite singer perform. She took me to the theater to watch a live play. One Christmas, she took me to a dinner party and introduced me to her friends.

"Grandmother always treated me with respect... even when I misbehaved."

They exchanged gifts and somehow, I ended up with a gift even though I had not brought one to exchange. Maybe somebody had an extra one or perhaps Grandmother brought two gifts to the party. But, being able to open a gift like all of the ladies made me feel special...liked an adult, even though I was the only child there.

Grandmother always treated me with respect...even when I misbehaved. She rarely whipped me, but whenever she promised to give me a whipping, she always kept her promise. She used a tiny belt (she called it her "strap") and would give me four or five whacks on my legs with it. The whacks did not hurt much, though my feelings suffered more than my legs.

She was always nice to me... "She's the sweetest one!" she would often say to me for no apparent reason. Whenever I yawned, she would say in a sweet voice, "Somebody's sleepy." I often woke up as early as five or six

A Gifted Child　　　　　　　*Dr. Grace LaJoy Henderson*
IN FOSTER CARE

o'clock in the morning when I visited Grandmother's house. Her favorite saying when she saw me up so early was, "The early bird catches the worms!"

She believed in speaking proper English and encouraged all of us to do the same. For example, she required us to address her as "Grandmother" instead of "Grandma." She made my sisters and brothers call me by my birth name of "Grace" instead of "Gracie." I didn't like that because I preferred "Gracie." It made me feel like I was special and loved by them.

Of all the children, I spent the most time at Grandmother's house. My father worked while my siblings were in school, and he asked Grandmother to babysit me. During those times, she often read books to me. At night time, she would make milkshakes in her blender and bring them to me in bed. Though she made all kinds -- vanilla and chocolate, I especially liked strawberry!

Sometimes, Grandmother took me to the second-hand store to buy clothes. She washed them right away when we returned home. She also ironed them and taught me to never wear wrinkled or "rough-dried" clothing. One day, Grandmother dressed me up in the cleaned second-hand clothes, washed, pressed, and styled my hair, then took

> *"Grandmother instilled in me the love of learning..."*

Grandmother　　　　21

A Gifted Child
IN FOSTER CARE

Dr. Grace LaJoy Henderson

me to have professional pictures taken. As a strong believer in education, Grandmother instilled in me the love of learning between the ages of two and five.

> *"She made everything a learning experience."*

She did this by only buying toys that helped me to learn, then played with the toys with me. She made *everything* a learning experience. Whenever we drove in the car, she spent most of the time pointing out things like street lights, signs, and explaining what certain colors meant. She would point to the stop sign and say to me, "s-t-o-p spells STOP."

It was Grandmother who taught me the alphabet, numbers, math, and how to read before I even started kindergarten. I started kindergarten when I was four years old even though the official age to begin was five. I had to take a test to get accepted into kindergarten early, and I passed the test thanks to my grandmother's diligence.

One day, when I was three or four years old, Grandmother told me I couldn't go outside to play until I learned how to write the alphabet. She had been teaching me the alphabet using educational toys and Sesame Street books, films and records. But on that day, she expected me to master what I had been learning.

I cried and begged to go outside, but she refused. I

A Gifted Child   *Dr. Grace LaJoy Henderson*
IN FOSTER CARE

had to learn to write both capital and small letters. I had some paper and sat in the high chair in her kitchen. Grandma had given me a Sesame Street book with the letters on it. I had to learn to write them without the book, so I worked and worked. When I didn't get it correct, she made me do it over and over. I practiced so many times and I wanted to go outside so badly. Lo and behold, I ended up writing the entire alphabet that day!

The first day of kindergarten class was quite scary. Grandmother told me what to expect, but I was still afraid to remain in the classroom without her there. Would the teacher be nice to me? Would the children like

> *"Would she abandon me the way my mother had?"*

me? But most of all, would Grandmother ever come back to pick me up? Would she abandon me the way my mother had? Finally, the teacher distracted me by showing me some interesting toys in the classroom.

While studying the toys, I looked up every now and then to see my Grandmother peeking at me, undoubtedly to see if I felt secure enough for her to leave. The final time I looked up, she was gone! I thought about crying, but by then I felt safe and didn't shed a tear.

After I started school, I stopped spending so much time over Grandmother's house. My father didn't need her to babysit me anymore.

A Gifted Child
IN FOSTER CARE

Dr. Grace LaJoy Henderson

Between kindergarten and second grade, I had my first experience with writing poetry. I took the poem "roses are red, violets are blue, sugar is sweet and so are you" and changed it in ways that I thought were more creative. Then I anxiously showed my classmates and teacher what I had done with the poem. When I saw how much they liked it, I felt proud of myself and tried other forms.

Today, I have to credit Grandmother with building a strong foundation within me, which enabled me to succeed in learning throughout my childhood.

While my father didn't need Grandmother's assistance as much after I started school, she continued to bring food to our house. We also visited her house for home-cooked meals on holidays such as Easter and Christmas. Thus, while Daddy struggled to raise six children alone, he could always depend on the never-ending assistance of Grandmother. Or so I thought.

4 - Left by Father

Through an unfortunate turn of events, Daddy discovered that, as a cement worker, the work was slow in Kansas City. He told us he planned to move to Florida where the weather was always nice and opportunities for work were plentiful. He would take my fifteen-year old brother with him, because he had been getting into trouble with children in the neighborhood. Daddy knew that if he left him, he could end up hurt, dead or in jail.

> *"...he left me and my other four siblings in a house alone."*

At that time, I was seven. When Daddy left, it was just me and the four older kids in a house alone. The oldest child was my fourteen-year old brother. My father asked his girlfriend Rose and my Aunt Mattie to check on us while he was gone. He also promised to send us money for food and bills on a weekly basis. I don't recall Grandmother coming around to help us during this time, but I don't know why.

Since Florida was a known vacation spot, my first thought was that my father was going to Florida to vacation. But, after he explained that the weather would allow him to have more opportunities to work, I understood a little better. Still, I wondered why he had to leave us. Knowing he made

A Gifted Child
IN FOSTER CARE
              Dr. Grace LaJoy Henderson

arrangements for people to check in on us and that he would send money helped ease my fears, but I never felt fully comfortable about him leaving. I guess that was because I looked to him for security and protection. But, because he was my father, I trusted his judgment and accepted the fact that he had to go.

    Things seemed to go well at first. One day, Aunt Mattie brought us some home-cooked food and quilts. Rose came over once to check on us. I even came home from school one day to discover that we had a few items of food and my sister and brother had fifty dollars. They told me they found the money under the floor in the attic. But, when I look back now, I believe my father sent the money as he had promised. They were just trying to trick me.

> *"...after a while, the money stopped and the lights, gas, water, and phone were turned off."*

    Nonetheless, even though a couple of people checked on us and it appears my father sent some money as he had promised, after a while, the money stopped and the lights, gas, water, and phone were turned off. Even the lock on the front door was broken, leaving me feeling very afraid. We also ran out of food.

    I went to school most days without breakfast, wear-

Left by Father

A Gifted Child   *Dr. Grace LaJoy Henderson*
IN FOSTER CARE

ing dirty clothes, and uncombed hair. One day my teacher's assistant combed my hair for me. I felt embarrassed about that when all of the other girls in my class came to school with their hair neatly combed. I also felt grateful and excited -- she was making me look pretty. Although I felt pretty that one day, things continued to get worse.

Rose never came back to check on us. Aunt Mattie never brought us more food. My two brothers began sleeping in shifts in front of the broken door to protect us from prowlers. The door lock had been broken by teenage boys from the neighborhood who broke into our house one night. They broke a window out in the back of the house also. My sister told me how they had a gun to her head that night. The boys threatened and taunted us because they knew we were in the house alone and had no parents. I was afraid to fall asleep every night.

I feared the boys coming back and hurting us. Maybe next time instead of my sister, it would be me. My brothers were afraid. Everything was gone. No food. No anything. Not even mayonnaise in the jar, or a potato to peel. We had been in the house for a few weeks and the situation became more desperate until one night I remember quite well.

Left by Father   27

A Gifted Child
IN FOSTER CARE

Dr. Grace LaJoy Henderson

Left by Father

A Gifted Child
IN FOSTER CARE

Dr. Grace LaJoy Henderson

5 - *Living in Foster Care*

One late night at about two o'clock, I was awakened by a sheriff. He told us, "We are taking you to an 'emergency foster home' for a nice hot breakfast." Those were the best words I had heard in weeks! I did not hesitate to go with them…I was hungry! I left the house without taking any belongings. In reality, I didn't have anything I wanted to take.

> *"We are going to take you to an 'emergency foster home' for a nice hot breakfast."*

We finally pulled up in front of the emergency foster home. It was a small house, but when we stepped inside the foster lady had cooked a large, hot breakfast in her very small kitchen. She prepared eggs, bacon, sausage, grits, pancakes, toast…the works! She went out of her way to get up at two o'clock in the morning to cook all of that food just for us.

After we ate, we slept there for the night. I felt happiness for the first time in a long time, and I fell into a deep, safe-feeling in my heart. Although we never knew who had called the authorities, it was the best thing anyone could have done for us.

A case worker picked us up the next morning to take us to a home that would be more permanent. Over time, I lived

Living in Foster Care   29

A Gifted Child
IN FOSTER CARE

Dr. Grace LaJoy Henderson

in three other foster homes. I don't remember much about my stay in the first two homes because I didn't live in them for very long. I do recall getting whipped and spanked a lot.

From there, I lived with Grandmother again for a brief period of time. During a court hearing, Grandmother agreed to take care of me and my sister, but in a just few days, my sister and I nearly destroyed her nice, clean home. While playing, we broke the seat off of her toilet stool and ripped a window shade in the bedroom we slept in. Although I believe Grandmother loved us, she couldn't deal with energetic children like us, especially since we had little home training.

She did not tell us how disappointed she was about us wrecking her home. But on the day we tore the shade, she helped us pack our bags, and had us sit on the porch until our caseworker came to pick us up. Eventually the caseworker arrived and took us from Grandmother's home to the home of "Big Mama." Her real name was Pearlie Mae Wiggins.

"Grandmother, in her distress, called the State Department of Social Services and demanded they pick us."

Big Mama revealed to me that Grandmother, in her distress, called the State Department of Social Services and demanded they pick us up immediately. She informed them we would be sitting on her porch with our things until they came.

A Gifted Child   *Dr. Grace LaJoy Henderson*
IN FOSTER CARE

Big Mama told me what my Grandmother had done because I constantly compared her to Grandmother, which made it difficult for me to accept Big Mama's authority. For instance, Big Mama gave me a white blouse to put on that had not been ironed. I looked at the blouse, saw it was wrinkled, and said to her, "*Grandmother* told me to never wear *rough-dried* clothing."

I had already informed Big Mama of several other things *Grandmother* taught me. It was my first day there and I could tell Big Mama was being especially patient with me. But when I said this, Big Mama looked at me with disappointment in her eyes. Undoubtedly, this irritated her to no end, but I felt Grandmother had taught me right. I guess I had a little bit of pride about it. Still I appreciated Big Mama telling me the truth about why I was no longer living with Grandmother.

While Grandmother never allowed me to take the educational books and toys she had bought me to my house when I lived with Daddy, she gave them to me when I moved to Big Mama's house. One toy I liked most was my "Show and Tell", which allowed me to see and hear stories by playing a record and viewing a slide show at the same time. In Big Mama's house, there was nowhere to put my "Show and Tell", so it had to be stored in the basement. Sadly, I never got to play with it throughout my stay in foster care.

Living in Foster Care   31

A Gifted Child
IN FOSTER CARE

Dr. Grace LaJoy Henderson

I lived with Big Mama for the next three years. When I look back, this was the only time in my young life that I experienced a stable home environment. She taught me how to cook, clean up, and care for myself, including my hair, my body, and my teeth. She made sure we had a full breakfast, lunch and dinner every day.

We celebrated every holiday to the fullest. On Thanksgiving and Christmas she cooked mega-meals with all the trimmings. I usually got what I wanted for Christmas. Every Fourth of July, she bought me new clothes and we went to a park and had a big picnic. For Easter, I got more new clothes and an Easter basket before we sat down to Big Mama's mega-meal. My foster father, Willie Wiggins or "Papa", would often take me to church and we usually went to church on Easter Sunday.

> *"...this is the only time in my young life that I experienced a stable home environment."*

Big Mama often placed me on punishment for misbehaving. Even with all of the good things she did for me, I *hated* those punishments.

Nonetheless, despite the punishments, Big Mama's home was the only home where I had an adult make sure I finished my homework. I even got placed in the Gifted and Talented Program at the elementary school I attended!

Living In Foster Care   32

A Gifted Child
IN FOSTER CARE

Dr. Grace LaJoy Henderson

However, I never understood why the school chose me for the "gifted" program. No one ever told me.

The day that I found out I had been chosen for the program, I had arrived at school late. I walked into my classroom and saw a boy sitting at a desk. "This is *my* desk!" I told him. When he insisted that it was *his* desk, I told my teacher. My teacher looked at me and smiled. Though I wondered why she was smiling when I was angry, she informed me that my desk

> *"...I never understood why the school chose me for the 'gifted' Program."*

had been moved. She then took me to its new location.

As we walked out of the classroom, I felt afraid. We walked together from the first floor to the second floor. My fear mounted. No one had prepared me for this! Finally, we walked into the new classroom and my teacher took me to my desk and said, "This is your desk and this is your new classroom." It was the Gifted and Talented classroom! I looked inside the desk and all of my school supplies were in it, so I was convinced that this was real.

At first, I felt nervous and unworthy to be in the gifted and talented class. I never felt as smart as the other children in that class. I believed they *deserved* to be there, but I did not. I did not tell my teacher how I felt, however, and I simply

Living in Foster Care

A Gifted Child
IN FOSTER CARE

Dr. Grace LaJoy Henderson

sat at my desk and began my new experience as one of the gifted and talented students.

I quickly found out the work was more challenging there than in my regular class. I was often afraid to speak up when I didn't understand the work. Learning had always been fun and easy for me, so this was an entirely new experience! I spent fourth and fifth grade in the same classroom and I got to know my classmates very well.

Big Mama told me I was the only foster child she ever had that was placed in the school's Gifted and Talented Program. The smile on her face when she told me made me feel like she was proud of me.

After living with Big Mama for about eighteen months, I saw my father again for the first time since he left me and my siblings in that house alone. He had been living in Florida. He visited the foster home and ate Christmas dinner with us. After dinner, Big Mama offered him a seat in her very immaculate, and clean, living room. She told him how well we were all doing and how smart I was. He could see that we lived in a clean home and that we were well cared for.

> *"...I saw my father again for the first time since he left me and my siblings in that house alone."*

Living In Foster Care   34

A Gifted Child
IN FOSTER CARE

Dr. Grace LaJoy Henderson

Before he left, he gave me and my sister some money and promised to bring us home with him. He lived in North Carolina at that time. Both my foster mother and my case worker always told me only good things about my father, so I could not wait for the day that he would finally get me out of foster care and take me home to live with him.

The weekend after my father's visit, Big Mama took my sister and me shopping for clothes with the money that my father had given us. I remember picking out some green wide-legged jeans and a matching blouse, which quickly became my favorite outfit! I even made sure I packed it to take with me when I finally went home to Daddy.

A Gifted Child
IN FOSTER CARE

Dr. Grace LaJoy Henderson

A Gifted Child
IN FOSTER CARE

Dr. Grace LaJoy Henderson

6 – Separated from Siblings

While living in foster care, I was separated from all my siblings except one of my sisters who also lived with Big Mama. I visited my other siblings three times during that three-year period. Excitement gripped me when I knew I was going to visit them.

My sister Danisha, who served in the United States Army, is three years older than me. She was always very neat and clean. Danisha lived with Big Mama at the same time as I did. I do not remember a lot about our relationship during foster care. She was very quiet. Throughout her life, she made good grades in school and she always got the jobs that she applied for. Today, she is a naturally gifted artist who has created some beautiful artwork.

My brother Terrance served in the United States Army. He is five years older than me. During foster care, Terrance started in the same foster home as my sister Carla and my brother Grayson, but ended up separated from them due to behavior issues. I once went to visit him in the Juvenile Detention Center and during that visit, he let me read some poetry he wrote.

Outside of foster care, Terrance often looked out for me. One day, when I was three years old, all of my siblings planned to walk to the park and I wanted to go. However, I

A Gifted Child
IN FOSTER CARE

Dr. Grace LaJoy Henderson

was not ready and didn't have anything clean to wear. I cried profusely as everyone told me, "You can't go."

Finally, Terrance turned back and said, "Come on Gracie." He took me upstairs and quickly found something for me to wear and took me to the park with everyone else. Terrance always showed a bit of favoritism toward me, and I remember feeling happy and appreciative of him. The fact that he took the time to help gave me a deep sense of hope and joy. Today, he has a gift for writing poetry and songs.

The United States Marines where my sister Carla served. She is six years older than me. Carla lived in the same foster home as my brother Grayson for the entire three years. They were moved to three or four different homes, but they remained together.

Carla was the first person to tell me I had a gift for writing. She told me, "Not everybody can write poems like that." She loved reading my poems and listening to me sing songs that I had written. This was another moment of feeling special and loved because she truly believed I had a gift. I didn't realize how her words impacted me, but when I look back I see it as a definitive moment that would lead me to the conviction that I could write.

My brother Grayson, who is seven years older than me, served in the United States Marines like Carla. Outside of foster care, he was a jokester who often shared funny stories

A Gifted Child   *Dr. Grace LaJoy Henderson*
IN FOSTER CARE

with the family. He also teased me a lot. Whenever he saw me crying he would make fun of me. However, he had a professional, business-like demeanor about himself and was always willing to give to those in need.

Danisha and I visited Grayson and Carla two times during our time in foster care. The first time we walked around the neighborhood with Carla. This was a big deal for me because Big Mama never allowed us to walk around the neighborhood that way.

Our second visit with Grayson and Carla included Terrance. Grandmother took us to her sister's house for a home cooked meal. She took some pictures of us, too. The only reason I remember this visit is because I have a copy of one of the pictures she took of us together that day. I feel fortunate to have it because it is the only picture I have of myself during my time in foster care.

Last, but not least, my oldest brother Jerome served in the United States Army. He had more influence on me than any of my other siblings. My father took Jerome with him when he left us in the house alone. Jerome remained with my father and I only saw him one time during my three years in foster care. The one time I saw him was when my father came to visit us at Big Mama's home.

"He taught me how to fistfight to ensure no one would ever hurt me."

Separated from Siblings   39

A Gifted Child
IN FOSTER CARE

Dr. Grace LaJoy Henderson

Outside of foster care, Jerome was very protective of me and did everything in his power to keep us from getting hurt by anything or anyone. He taught me how to fistfight to ensure no one would ever hurt me. He would flex his arm muscle and tell me to hit his arm as hard as I could. After I hit as hard as I could, he would say, "That's not hard enough! Hit me harder!"

I realized he wanted me to win a fight if I ever had one. But, it was fun to hit his arm. In my mind, I was thinking I was going to lay him in the dust. But his mission was to help me prepare for some of the hard knocks he knew I would face in the neighborhoods we lived in. Because of these boxing lessons, I was prepared for any adversary.

Jerome was also a go-getter! He wanted to make something good of himself. In his determination, he gained much knowledge and never hesitated to share it with others, which impressed us all.

I purposely did not talk in this book about how each of my siblings was affected by being separated from our mother, father, and each other. They can share their own story, if they wish, much better than I can. Like any family in such a situation, each of was affected differently but we have stayed together as a family through it all.

I believe our birth order played a big part in the way

A Gifted Child
IN FOSTER CARE

Dr. Grace LaJoy Henderson

we were affected. For example, Jerome, being the oldest, knew our mother longer than any of us and he saw a lot more of our parents' struggles. He also has a clearer picture of how their struggles affected each of us. I, on the other hand, being the youngest, did not see much of their relationship. Although I remember some things, I have had to ask a lot of questions and rely on the stories of other people to find out about my parents' struggles and the events leading up to my mother leaving.

Even though I was separated from my siblings, each of them influenced me greatly while I grew up. So, while Big Mama and Papa took care of my needs when I lived in foster care, my brothers and sisters played a unique role in looking out for me and impacting my life outside of foster care.

A Gifted Child
IN FOSTER CARE

Dr. Grace LaJoy Henderson

7 – A Typical Day in Foster Care

There were four girls living in Big Mama's house: me, my sister Danisha, and my two foster sisters, Laura and Tina. Other girls came and left after very short periods of time. But the four of us were there together the entire time. I also had a foster brother named Robert. He was placed in Big Mama's care at birth and she eventually adopted him.

Our space was upstairs. It was an open area with four beds, a large dresser, a large chest of drawers, and two closets. Everyone had their own drawer and closet space. Tina and I shared the large chest of drawers and the smaller

"We all had specific daily chores."

closet. Danisha and Laura used the tall dresser and the larger closet. Danisha and Laura were very neat, but Big Mama corrected Tina and me regularly for not cleaning up correctly.

We all had specific daily chores. Mine were making my bed, keeping my part of the upstairs clean, cleaning the bathroom, dusting the shined hardwood floors in the living and dining room areas, feeding the dogs, and cleaning Papa's spit bucket. Papa chewed tobacco and had a special bucket that he spit his tobacco in throughout the day. I had to get the bucket out of their bedroom, pour the spit into the toilet, and wash it out using a disinfectant. Then, I would fill the bucket about

A Gifted Child
IN FOSTER CARE

Dr. Grace LaJoy Henderson

half full with water, pour about a capful of disinfectant into the water, and put the bucket back in their room on Papa's side of the bed.

On certain days I hung clean clothes from the washing machine out to dry. With clothes pins in hand, I placed them on clothes lines in the basement or in the backyard. When the clothes were dry, I folded them.

Mornings at Big Mama's house were rather challenging. Big Mama was a light sleeper and did not like being awakened before she was ready to get up in the morning. Sometimes as we prepared for school, we would make too much noise and wake her up.

> *"If Big Mama wasn't happy, nobody was happy."*

Whenever that happened, a bad mood followed. If Big Mama wasn't happy, nobody was happy. To keep from waking her up, we walked as lightly as we could on the very squeaky upstairs floors.

After tip-toeing for about twenty minutes, we all went downstairs for breakfast. Laura and Danisha prepared either oatmeal or egg sandwiches for everyone. Oatmeal made me sick to my stomach and I usually had to go to the bathroom and throw up whenever I ate it. I always wondered if it was the cinnamon Laura put in the oatmeal that made me get sick.

A Gifted Child   Dr. Grace LaJoy Henderson
IN FOSTER CARE

This frustrated Big Mama greatly, and she finally told me I could not eat breakfast anymore. I suspect she thought I was pretending to be sick because I just did not want to eat my breakfast. Thus, even when Laura and Danisha cooked egg sandwiches, I still couldn't have breakfast.

"Breakfast makes you sick," Big Mama told me, when I asked if I could have an egg sandwich. This angered me, and I felt deprived every morning that I was refused breakfast. I thought it was unfair. Still, I made up for the loss of breakfast at dinner time. I don't remember much about lunch, but Big Mama *always* let me have dinner. And after about three weeks, she allowed me to have breakfast again.

After breakfast, we walked to school. I loved going to school. The things I liked most about school were going to the school library, playing kickball at recess, and going on field trips. At the school library, I checked out books that were easy to read. I had no interest in chapter books because it took too long to get to the ending. I liked to know as soon as possible how the story worked out. I didn't care for all of
the detail and drama in longer books. Deep down, I didn't feel like I read as fast as other students.

> *"At the school library, I checked out books that were easy to read."*

A Typical Day in Foster Care   45

A Gifted Child
IN FOSTER CARE

Dr. Grace LaJoy Henderson

I liked playing kickball, but I was usually one of the last ones chosen by the team captain. That made me feel a bit rejected, but at least I got picked at the end.

Sometimes my teacher took me and my class on outings away from the school. We went to the zoo, the museum, on a picnic at the park, and to the public library. The librarian taught us how to find books according to the filing system. The library field trip was most memorable because the librarian helped us obtain a library card and encouraged everyone to check out at least one book. She also taught us the importance of returning library books on time.

> *"I often had to explain that Tina was my "foster" sister and Danisha was my real sister."*

During the school day, other children often asked me if Danisha and Tina were my sisters. They were surprised when I said they were, because Danisha was much sweeter and quieter than me, and Tina and I did not look anything alike. I often had to explain that Tina was my "foster" sister and Danisha was my real sister.

After school, Tina, Danisha, and I would walk home together. Danisha and I went to the same school for only one year before she moved on to junior high school. Then Tina and I walked home together alone.

A Typical Day in Foster Care 46

A Gifted Child
IN FOSTER CARE

Dr. Grace LaJoy Henderson

Every evening, the first thing I did when I came home from school was go upstairs and get started on my homework. Then I ate dinner, fed the dogs, did my chores, played outside, took my bath, combed my hair, and got my clothes ready for school the next day.

"...the first thing I did when I came home from school was go upstairs and get started on my homework."

I could not wait for Big Mama to come to the bottom of the stairs and say the three words I looked forward to hearing every evening, "Ya'll can eat!" That meant a full course dinner which included food from all the four food groups, plus Kool-Aid. We would race to the bathroom, wash our hands, go the kitchen, fix our plates, and sit at the kitchen table together and eat.

As I walked into the kitchen to eat, Big Mama carried two plates of food into her bedroom. They were for herself and Papa. Sometimes, as we sat at the kitchen table eating, Big Mama would call out from her room "Gracilee!" -- the nick name she gave me -- "Bring me an onion." She loved onions and ate them with all of her meals.

After dinner, we all put the bones and scraps from our plate in the "dog bucket", a red bucket which sat in the kitchen. Papa mixed the food from the "dog bucket" with store-bought

A Typical Day in Foster Care   47

A Gifted Child Dr. Grace LaJoy Henderson
IN FOSTER CARE

dog food, then fed it to his hunting dogs. He taught me how to feed the dogs and that became one of my chores. When my chores were done, I played outside until I had to get ready for the next school day. I had to be in the house by seven o'clock and in bed by nine.

While outside during the early part of the evening, I often rode my bike. Big Mama didn't let us ride far because she didn't want anything bad to happen to me or any of her girls. Towards the latter part of the evening, I caught frogs and lightning bugs. I put the frogs in covered jars with holes in the lid and grass for food. I pulled the lights off the lightning bugs and attached them on my ears as if I had light-up earrings.

When playtime was over, I went in the house, took my bath and washed out the tub. Then I combed my hair and put a scarf over my hair-do so it would be neat when I got up the next morning. As I lay in bed trying to go to sleep, I felt safe and looked forward to the next day.

A Gifted Child
IN FOSTER CARE

Dr. Grace LaJoy Henderson

8 – How Foster Care Shaped My Life

As I think about my typical day in foster care, I realize my foster parents sacrificed a lot for us. The structure instilled in my life during that time is what caused me to be identified, by my school, as a gifted student. Foster care met the basic needs of my social, physical, mental, and emotional well-being.

> *"Foster care met the basic needs of my social, physical, mental, and emotional well-being."*

Before foster care I had no real structure. Our family rarely participated in outside activities together. I had no special chores, and no specific bedtime. I did not experience a consistent flow of discipline.

During foster care, Big Mama took us to the drive in. Papa took us fishing and taught me how to clean and scale fish. They showed me how to work in the vegetable and flower gardens and how to do yard work. Although I hated Big Mama's punishments, I can now appreciate that she took the time to enforce the rules.

Before foster care, I never went to the doctor or dentist. But, during foster care, my caseworker took me to the doctor and dentist for regular checkups. The first time I went to the dentist I had seven cavities. The dentist filled

A Gifted Child
IN FOSTER CARE

Dr. Grace LaJoy Henderson

them all.

Before foster care, I never received brand new clothes or shoes. One day I came home from school to find Big Mama sitting on the couch in the dining room sorting through a big box of brand new clothes inside a department store box. She distributed the clothes to us. That was the first time in my life I ever received new clothes, and so many of them! After that, she continued to provide new clothes every Fourth of July, Easter, and Christmas.

Outside of foster care, my favorite part of the school day was lunch because I was not fully nourished at home. While in foster care, I was well fed, except during that period of time when I had to miss breakfast because "breakfast made me sick."

Big Mama gave me constant and consistent discipline. At home, there was more leniency when it came to discipline. In foster care, I was taught the proper way to do chores and rules were strictly enforced. Outside of foster care, I was never taught how to do chores. Daddy told me to clean up, but he never taught me how to do it correctly. Grandmother kept a clean home, but never made me clean. She cleaned up after me and did all the work herself.

Even though Grandmother instilled the love of learning in me at an early age, I was not recognized as being gifted before foster care. While in foster care, I never

A Gifted Child   *Dr. Grace LaJoy Henderson*
IN FOSTER CARE

appreciated all the good things Big Mama did for me. I was only focused on the strict discipline and punishments that she administered, and I was angry about them. But when I look back, I can clearly see and appreciate the stable home environment, family activities, attention, health and dental care, and discipline I received while in foster care. These elements built the foundation of stability in my life that I enjoy today.

A Gifted Child
IN FOSTER CARE

Dr. Grace LaJoy Henderson

9 - Life After Foster Care

When I was ten years old, the summer after I completed fifth grade, my father finally met all of the state requirements to become eligible to bring my siblings and me home to live with him. He sent us bus tickets. As I was packing to leave Big Mama's house, I wanted to take my "Show and Tell" with me, but she told me there would be no room on the bus for it. Sadly, I ended up leaving without it. I felt extremely disappointed because I had waited three years to play with it. Grandmother never let me take the toys she bought me to Daddy's house because she knew they'd get torn up. So now was my big chance, but it was not to be.

My two sisters and I rode the bus from Kansas City, Missouri, to Charlotte, North Carolina, where we were to be reunited with Daddy and our three brothers. After an extremely long twenty-three-hour bus ride, we finally reached the bus station in Charlotte, North Carolina, where my father stood waiting. My brothers were not with him, but it was refreshing to see my father. I knew the three-year separation was finally over.

> *"The first place my father took us was to meet his girlfriend, Ms. Ruby, ... "*

The first place my father took us was to meet his girlfriend, Ms. Ruby, whom he had

A Gifted Child
IN FOSTER CARE

Dr. Grace LaJoy Henderson

known for a number of years. Ms. Ruby was small-statured and had a cute, soft voice. She treated me with love and respect from the first day that I met her. After the meeting, my father took us to the three-bedroom townhome where we would be living. My brothers were there, but I remember little of our reunion. I only recall my father showing us the upstairs bedrooms.

The largest bedroom was my father's. My brothers had the second, and the third was shared by my sisters and me. Carla had her own twin size bed, while Danisha and I shared the second twin size bed.

We had everything we needed that summer. My father usually cooked breakfast, especially on weekends. He left for work before I woke up in the mornings during the week. He also prepared dinner in the evenings. There was *nothing* that we needed that he did not provide during that time. He even took us shopping for school clothes just before the first day of school.

I started sixth grade in Charlotte, North Carolina, but before that year was over, we moved back to Kansas City, Missouri, then to Detroit, Michigan. Daddy moved to wherever the cement work was.

During the summer before I entered seventh grade, we moved back to Charlotte, North Carolina, where Danisha and I lived with my father and his girlfriend. By then, all of my

A Gifted Child
IN FOSTER CARE

Dr. Grace LaJoy Henderson

other siblings had entered the military. From sixth grade until eighth grade my father moved us back and forth several times between Charlotte, Kansas City, and Detroit.

"...I went to school with gangsters and students who carried guns and knives, ... "

As we moved from place to place, oftentimes we dwelled within the inner-city area. This meant I went to school with gangsters and students who carried guns and knives, a situation that challenged me repeatedly. As the "new kid" I had to work harder at building relationships with my schoolmates. I was not always accepted at the start, but I would always meet at least one or two other children who were interested in being friends. On the other hand, there always seemed to be someone at school who wanted to fight me for one reason or another.

For instance, when I was the "new girl" at one neighborhood middle school, a girl named "Tracy" wanted to fight me. She admitted I had not done anything to her, but she was jealous because I "took all her boyfriends." Just for the record, I had no interest in any of those guys, but they found me attractive as the "new girl" and attempted to get to know me better.

One day Tracy began telling people she was going to beat me up after school. That afternoon, I walked home with

Life After Foster Care

A Gifted Child
IN FOSTER CARE

Dr. Grace LaJoy Henderson

a friend, "Lisa", who offered to help me if a fight occurred. As Lisa and I strolled home, we looked back and saw Tracy behind us, and she was not alone. Gang members from a very popular all-girl gang followed her. I was nervous. I thought I might be able to handle Tracy, but I feared those gang members.

As the gang got closer and closer to Lisa and me, Lisa's father arrived in his car and took her away. Before they drove away, she asked her father if he could give me a ride home because I just lived around the corner, but he was not willing to take me home.

Within seconds of Lisa leaving, Tracy and the gang appeared in front of me ready to fight. Tracy jumped in front of me prepared to sling punches. But before anyone was hit, the gang leader leaped in front of Tracy and pushed her! To my surprise, the gang followed Tracy because they wanted to fight *her*, not help her fight *me*! The gang leader told me to go home and I did. I was so scared and now I felt totally relieved. I went home with a skip in my step, thinking I'd had some good luck for once. Maybe there was someone up there watching over me!

Although I escaped that time, there were other situations where I was forced to fight. One day I came home

> *"When two people fight, nobody wins!"*

Life After Foster Care   56

A Gifted Child   Dr. Grace LaJoy Henderson
IN FOSTER CARE

from school with my hair messed up and my clothing out of whack; I had gotten into a fight with a girl on the way home from school. When I saw Daddy's concern, I told him what happened. "I won," I said. I thought that would impress him and he would be proud of me. Instead he angrily said, "You did not win *anything*! When two people fight, *nobody* wins!"

I did not get into fights in foster care like I had after going to live with my father. I believe it was because in foster care I lived in a stable home for three years, which gave me the time to develop secure friendships with my classmates. However, when I went to live with my father, we moved around a lot, which made it difficult to develop any friendships before we moved again. As a result, I never had stability in my young life after foster care.

Life After Foster Care   57

A Gifted Child
IN FOSTER CARE

Dr. Grace LaJoy Henderson

10 – Daddy Left Again

About two and a half years after my father got us out of foster care, he left us again! I was thirteen years old. *This time* he left my sisters and me to live with a lady in North Carolina. All three of my brothers had gone to the military by this time. This lady was not one of Daddy's girlfriends. She was simply an older lady who he entrusted to look out for us until we could find a place of our own, while he traveled looking for cement work.

Before Daddy left again, he gave my eighteen-year old sister, Carla, specific instructions about how to provide for me and Danisha without him. She found a townhome for us to live in that charged rent according to our income. Since we did not have any income, we paid nothing for rent.

> *"...my life was threatened when I was thirteen years old."*

We moved into the townhome during my eighth-grade year and I began riding the school bus to the junior high school. I met many children at school and in the townhome complex that I lived in. I also had many experiences, both good and bad, while living with my sisters. Of all the things that happened, the scariest experience was the time my life was threatened when I was thirteen years old. Here is how it

A Gifted Child
IN FOSTER CARE

Dr. Grace LaJoy Henderson

happened:

After one o'clock in the morning, I walked home from a YMCA dance party with "Ron", a fifteen-year-old boy. Ron was not my boyfriend; he simply offered to walk home with me because I did not have a ride and I was afraid to go home alone. Ron had a ride home, but the car he went in did not have enough room for me, so he got out of the car to walk with me. We lived in the same townhome complex. Initially, I stayed on the outside of the road, which did not have a sidewalk.

Suddenly, a car drove past really fast! It scared me so much that Ron offered to take the outside of the road so that I could be safer. The next car that drove by hit him! I watched in horror as Ron's body was thrown in the air by the car, and then crashed to the ground. The car sped off without even slowing down.

In my disbelief, I expected him to stand up and say something like, "Boy, these drivers are crazy!" But, he did not move. As I looked closer, I realized his body had been broken to pieces. Bones stuck out of his legs and arms. I panicked and became totally hysterical!

I ran alone through a funeral home parking lot and a wooded area to get to the townhomes where we lived! My plan was to tell his family what I had just witnessed. When I reached our townhome complex, a couple of people stopped

A Gifted Child
IN FOSTER CARE

Dr. Grace LaJoy Henderson

me to ask what was wrong. "The car went up in the air!" I said hysterically as I continued to run to Ron's home.

His mother came to the door and saw the fearful and hysterical state I was in. I told her Ron had been hit by a car and she immediately started crying and praying for her son. She prayed as she followed me to the scene of the accident, "God, please don't let it be anything serious!" she pleaded. As I listened to her prayer, I knew in my heart it was too late because I had already seen his broken body lying on the ground.

After being in the hospital for thirty days, Ron's family was forced to make the devastating decision to pull the plug on the life support equipment. Ron did not survive this terrible accident! I was too afraid to attend the funeral and continued to be fearful for many years after the accident. I experienced "survivors guilt" whenever I thought about the fact that had I stayed on the outside of the road, it would have been *me* who got hit by the car instead of him.

Today, I refuse to walk on the edge of the road even when I am on a sidewalk. Over the years, I have often reflected on that scary, life-changing experience. I am saddened by the unexpected loss of Ron's life. I believe there is a supernatural reason why my life was spared on that road - - perhaps so I could one day realize my purpose and use my gift to inspire and empower other people.

Daddy Left Again

A Gifted Child
IN FOSTER CARE

Dr. Grace LaJoy Henderson

It was soon after that experience that several people noticed I had gift for writing. Once in eighth grade, my English teacher noted my creative writing ability and complimented me in front of the entire class. Since there was a boy in that class that I had a crush on, it made the teacher's compliment more meaningful to me.

> *"...my English teacher noted my creative writing ability..."*

As part of the English curriculum, my teacher often asked the students to write different types of stories. She read them, graded them, and returned our papers to us. One day, after she had handed our papers back to us, she mentioned that there was one student in the class who wrote an exceptional story. That student was me! She went on to say that she loved to read my stories because she always looked forward to my creative endings.

When I was thirteen, Carla read a poem I wrote about a boy I liked. The poem was entitled "Watching You" and it is the first poem I actually kept. She reiterated the idea that I had a gift. From that time on, I began to share my poetry, songs, raps and stories with friends and family. They often asked if they could have a copy of whatever the piece was at the time. "I can't give

> *"...I'm going to write a book one day"*

Daddy Left Again

A Gifted Child
IN FOSTER CARE

Dr. Grace LaJoy Henderson

you a copy because I'm going to write a book one day", I would always say.

I was still living with Carla when I started high school. There, I continued to be recognized for my creative talent. One day my acting teacher shared some kind thoughts about me and my work with all of the students in the class.

"...after leaving foster care, my grades dropped and I was never again recognized by any school system for having good grades or for being a 'gifted' student."

Even though my creative talent was noticed, after leaving foster care, my grades dropped and I was never again recognized by any school system for having good grades or for being a "gifted" student. I believe this happened because after foster care I no longer had anyone who encouraged me to do my homework.

Although, my father was not with me during this time, he had frequently told me I was "hard-headed" whenever I misbehaved. He meant I was defiant, disobedient and incapable of obeying his instructions. The interesting part about it was I believed him! It was during my high school years in North Carolina that I first realized I was not "hard-headed", which had hurt me so much in those early years.

Daddy Left Again   63

A Gifted Child   *Dr. Grace LaJoy Henderson*
IN FOSTER CARE

Here is how I came to that realization: I was sent to the principal's office because I disobeyed the school's behavior policy. The principal noticed something special about me. He said I had decent grades and that I seemed to have a lot of friends, so he did not understand why I had disobeyed. When he asked me why, I responded, "It's because I'm hard-headed."

After I said that, the principal stared at me with disbelief. To convince him I said, "Really, that is what my daddy always told me, so that is why I have always disobeyed." With compassion in his eyes, a look that is printed deeply in my memory, his head going back and forth as if to say "no". I sensed he was looking at me as if to say, "You poor thing, you have been wounded and that needs to be corrected right now." So the principal said, "No, you are not hard-headed." For some reason, I just believed him! So, from that day on, I believed my Daddy was wrong about that issue.

I always believed Daddy had good intentions and would never say anything to me that he knew would hurt me or destroy my self-esteem. Sometimes parents say things, I think, that they don't realize have a great impact on their children. Even though he made some mistakes, I still remember many of his wise sayings. He often said, "I'm not

A Gifted Child
IN FOSTER CARE

Dr. Grace LaJoy Henderson

going to always be around." He said this when he taught us the things we needed to do to take care of ourselves. He knew he would soon be traveling to his next destination, without us. So, he wanted to make sure we would be able to manage while he was not around.

> *"...he wanted to make sure we would be able to manage while he was not around."*

After Daddy left this time, I lived with Carla from eighth to eleventh grade.

A Gifted Child
IN FOSTER CARE

Dr. Grace LaJoy Henderson

Daddy Left Again

11 – Pregnant at Seventeen

I was in the eleventh grade and still attending high school in North Carolina when Carla moved to Kansas City. My brother Grayson had been discharged from the Marines by then, so he moved into the townhome. I ended up moving to Kansas City to live with Carla again during the summer after I completed eleventh grade.

Just before I was to begin my senior year of high school, I did not have any decent clothes to wear. So, my brother Jerome took me shopping. He allowed me to pick out some outfits that I liked, and purchased them for me with his own money.

I began my senior year in Kansas City. During that year, my father returned and moved into the one bedroom apartment where I lived with my two sisters.

I won Homecoming Queen that year. My father did not attend the homecoming ceremony, but when I got home, he jumped up from his comfortable chair and put on a three-piece suit just to take a picture with me wearing my homecoming robe and crown.

"I continued to use my creative writing skills that year, ..."

I continued to use my creative writing skills that year, as I entered two poems in a poetry contest. One of them won

A Gifted Child
IN FOSTER CARE

Dr. Grace LaJoy Henderson

"...I ended up becoming pregnant during the summer immediately after graduation."

third place and the other received an honorable mention. This was the year I wrote the most poems about boys. Some of the poems I wrote back then did not portray the inspiration and empowerment my poetry portrays today. Nevertheless, I continued to write anyway and by the middle of my senior year, I had a collection of about seventy or eighty poems.

One day, I unknowingly left my collection of poems in my home economics classroom. I did not realize I left them until one day while sitting in my economics class, my teacher held up the stack of poems and asked "who wrote this poem about 'Life'?" When I told her those were my poems, she looked at me with a proud smile on her face and said, "You *do* have talent, don't you?"

During the last days of my senior year, leading up to graduation, several of my teachers wished me luck with my writing. But after graduation, I did not pursue a career in writing. In fact, I ended up becoming pregnant during the summer immediately after graduation.

The boy was a friend I knew from high school. I used to tell him I was going to have a little girl by him, joking, of course. He would blush and say, "No way." But that summer,

Pregnant at Seventeen

A Gifted Child
IN FOSTER CARE

Dr. Grace LaJoy Henderson

we talked more and spent time alone together. When we talked about sex, I had a lot of fear. But in time, I got pregnant. I had wanted a baby since I was thirteen.

I wanted somebody who would love me no matter what. Becoming a mother was the answer. I believed my baby would love me unconditionally. So, I wanted to get pregnant and I was happy to be pregnant. I remember thinking if I was going to get pregnant by anybody, I was happy it was him because he was a pretty good guy. I didn't have a clue at that time how tough being a single parent would be.

At the end of my senior year, I had secured my first job at a fast food restaurant. I did not have a car and my working hours were in the evening, so, it would be dark outside when I got off work. My brother Jerome told me, "You should not be riding the bus at night time, especially being pregnant!" He began picking me up on the nights I worked. I was seventeen years old at that time.

Still pregnant, I began attending a local community college in the fall of 1984. I dropped out of college when I was eighteen years old to give birth to my beautiful baby girl, whom I named Arica Nicole. Nonetheless, I returned to college afterwards and earned a clerical science certificate. By the time I gave birth to Arica at age eighteen, I had moved out of my sister's apartment and began living in an apartment on my own.

A Gifted Child
IN FOSTER CARE

Dr. Grace LaJoy Henderson

My baby's father had gotten a job that caused him to travel when I was about one month pregnant. Then he went into the Navy. I met his mother, Easter Mae Henderson, during this time, and she vowed immediately to help me. She told me if I needed *anything* I could ask her for it and she would provide it for me. "If you can name it, you can claim it!" she assured me. She kept every promise she made to be there and provide for me. I know I could not have made it without her help.

She was at the hospital with me during my very difficult delivery. After I was released from the hospital, I could barely walk. She took me into her home and took care of me. She did everything from preparing my baby's bottles to cooking and serving me breakfast, lunch, and dinner daily until my body was healed and I was able to care for myself and my baby. After I regained my strength, I took Arica and went back to the apartment I was renting.

I moved into that apartment while I was pregnant, but I never really lived in it because I went back to stay with my sister until I gave birth. On my first night back in the apartment with my new baby, I discovered it was infested with mice. I was afraid of mice, and I certainly did not want my baby living in such an environment. That night, I left the apartment with my baby and ended up living with "Peaches" (Arica's father's sister), who took care of me until I found another apartment.

A Gifted Child
IN FOSTER CARE

Dr. Grace LaJoy Henderson

I finally found another apartment, but during my first night living there, people outside spoke loudly and cussed a lot. That morning, I woke up and heard a couple of men outside my front door gambling with dice and cussing. I quickly realized this was an unsafe, drug-infested environment and not

> *"I quickly realized this was an unsafe, drug infested environment and not right for my new baby."*

right for my new baby. I did not move out, perhaps because I was tired of moving. Instead, I just began praying for a clean, quiet, safe place to live as soon as possible.

It took six months, but finally an apartment manager gave me some favor. She had informed me that there was a two-year waiting list and the apartment complex generally only catered to low-income individuals who were retired and had no children. But she made an exception and allowed me to move in after being on the waiting list for only six months. I moved into the apartment with my seven-month-old daughter and lived there for seven years.

My father, who had been living with his girlfriend in North Carolina, came to live with me and my daughter for about two months. He and his girlfriend had broken up. I felt happy though a bit uncomfortable about him living with me. I had struggled without parents for so many years and now my father needed to live with me until he found a place of his own. It was during his stay that I realized I did not really know a lot about this man that I called "Daddy". He felt like a stranger in many ways.

Feeling uncomfortable, I asked my apartment manager if she had an apartment available for him. She had a one-bedroom apartment open at the time. And since Daddy was a senior citizen, just over sixty years old, he was a perfect candidate for an apartment in the building. He lived there for about three months before he moved back to North Carolina to reunite with his girlfriend.

After Daddy moved back to North Carolina, he died at sixty-seven years old. While he lived, I often thought, "Even though I love Daddy, when he dies I probably won't miss him a whole lot. It will feel as if he is just out of town like he had been for most of my life." Still, I feel honored that he lived with me and had the opportunity to hold Arica in his arms before he left the earth.

In addition to this experience with my father, several other things happened during my stay in that apartment with my daughter. I began working seasonally for the federal government, got married, had a second child named Aric Jamal, got divorced, and went back to college. But, most importantly, during that time, I started to grow spiritually and began volunteering at my local church.

A Gifted Child
IN FOSTER CARE

Dr. Grace LaJoy Henderson

While becoming pregnant after my senior year resulted in some difficult times for me, I learned I could still be successful in life. Becoming pregnant forced me to quit college, but it did not stop me from returning to college later to eventually earn my Doctorate in Christian Counseling. My strength and determination became a source of inspiration for my two children. My diligence in returning to college, in spite of challenges, empowered my children to know that they, too, could go to college. My diligence also empowered *me* to know my children could go to college and become successful!

I believe now that if I had remained in foster care until I was eighteen, I would not have become a mother at the time I did. Outside of foster care, I had too much freedom to do whatever I wanted to do. But, inside of foster care, I received clear and regular discipline. That discipline would have kept me out of trouble and prevented me from becoming pregnant at seventeen.

A Gifted Child
IN FOSTER CARE

Dr. Grace LaJoy Henderson

A Gifted Child
IN FOSTER CARE

Dr. Grace LaJoy Henderson

12 – My Gift Revealed

Although I was never recognized for being "gifted" after leaving foster care, my gift of writing kept coming back to me in various ways. I first recognized it while raising my children as a single parent. When I finally began counting, I discovered over two hundred poems, thirty-five songs and three stage plays that I created.

It's funny, because before I knew writing was my gift, I often wondered, "What is my gift?" even though I had boxes full of creative things I had written!

"She told me that I could be 'the next Maya Angelou', the famous poet."

In thinking back about this time when I had no idea what my gift was, I am reminded of this story: One day, in my search for a job, I went to the unemployment office. The unemployment specialist who assisted me saw something special in me. She told me that I could be "the next Maya Angelou", a famous poet.

The amazing part about it was she didn't even know I wrote poems! She invited me to speak to a group of girls that she worked with in her spare time! But even with her insight, it still did not occur to me that writing could be my gift.

While I worked here and there, I often shared my writing with others. People began to tell me they felt

A Gifted Child
IN FOSTER CARE   *Dr. Grace LaJoy Henderson*

empowered by my writing and could relate to the messages in it. After receiving numerous compliments from people who were inspired by my writing, I finally began to think writing was my special gift. Knowing my writing was a source of inspiration for other people, I decided to share it with the world, but I had no idea where to begin.

At that time, I worked with children at the church I attended. I volunteered as children's church worker, youth leader, Sunday school teacher, vacation bible school teacher and youth drama department director. I also assisted in many other areas as needed.

> *"...I ended up writing and publishing my first book of poetry."*

While volunteering with the youth, I took the position of Youth Drama Director and produced, staged and directed all three of the stage plays that I had written. I even used some of the songs I wrote in two of the plays.

As I worked in these areas, I began researching book publishing. A few years later, I ended up writing and publishing my first book of poetry. After I finished the book, I sent a copy to my friend Nena, whom I had not spoken with in over twenty years. We reconnected again after she received the book and she shared her memories of how I used

My Gift Revealed   76

A Gifted Child
IN FOSTER CARE

Dr. Grace LaJoy Henderson

to make up funny raps and creatively change words to popular songs in a way that made her laugh. She had no idea my silly actions back then would result in my writing gift twenty years later!

> *"She had no idea that my silly actions back then would result in my writing gift twenty years later!"*

Since publishing the poetry book, I have written and published numerous books and CDs. I have also helped other writers to become authors. One lady who was well over eighty years old at the time, became a new author after I helped her write and publish her autobiography.

Just as my friend Nena had no idea that a silly-acting girl like me would end up doing such great things, neither did my foster mother who said, "You never know how children are going to turn out when they are young", after reading one of my books.

> *"...being abandoned by my mother and father and living in foster care are what shaped me into the person I am today;"*

Today, I wake up around six o'clock every morning, excited about getting up and working on the thing I am passionate about -- writing. It's like what Grandmother use to say to me, "The early bird catches the worms".

My Gift Revealed

A Gifted Child
IN FOSTER CARE

Dr. Grace LaJoy Henderson

I often wonder what my life would have been like if my mother had not left. Perhaps things would have been better. But then I am reminded that events such as being abandoned by my mother and father and living in foster care are what shaped me into the person I am today; and today I like the person I've become.

Even though I only lived in foster care for three years, the stable environment it offered taught me how to obtain and maintain the sense of security that is apparent in my life today. The punishments while in foster care that I hated so much, are what instilled the discipline I need today to create my vision, accomplish my goals, walk in my passion, and fulfill my purpose.

Being chosen for the Gifted and Talented Program as a foster child taught me that I can be successful in the midst of turmoil. It taught me that I was destined for greatness regardless of my circumstances.

If my life story had been different, then I would most likely be a totally different person and I would have never had the opportunity to experience being *a gifted child in foster care*.

A Gifted Child　　　　　　*Dr. Grace LaJoy Henderson*
IN FOSTER CARE

13 – *Empowerment for Children*

Whether you are in foster care or not, you have been affected by the choices of someone else. My mother's choice to leave impacted my life both negatively and positively. Negatively, because it hurt very badly and I had to struggle to overcome feelings of fear, insecurity and rejection. Positively, because I ended up writing to deal with those feelings and my writing ended up helping other people.

In the same way other people's choices affect your life, *your* choices affect the lives of *others*. Knowing my choice to write this book would affect others, I was careful not to speak negatively of those who impacted my life regardless of whether their impact was positive or negative.

During pre-publication of this book, several reviewers suggested, "You should share more details about the negative experiences in your life." Like many children in foster care, I experienced physical, mental, and emotional abuse. Those things will always be a part of my past, but in order to walk in my successful future I had to let go of my painful past.

Don't get me wrong, I was very angry when I left foster care. For thirty years, I dwelled on all of the

Empowerment for Children   79

A Gifted Child
IN FOSTER CARE

Dr. Grace LaJoy Henderson

negative, hurtful things. But, whenever I thought about a stable home environment, regular health care, good physical hygiene, learning to cook, and proper housekeeping I went back to foster care. Whenever I thought about being "smart" or "gifted" I remembered foster care.

The more I dwelled on these positive things, the more I was able to truly let go of the negative experiences, which released forgiveness in my heart. I had to forgive everyone who abandoned, rejected, or mistreated me. Forgiving meant no more talking, writing, or complaining about my negative past, but sharing and showing the positive things that have resulted from it.

As you begin recognizing and utilizing your gifts and talents, remember this: You cannot see in front if you are looking behind. So, the best way to start moving forward is to refrain from looking back. Your life experiences, good and bad, have power. If used effectively, your life experiences will do two things: Make you stronger and empower others.

Here are three things you can do to use your life experiences effectively: Recognize your power; be confident; take advantage of opportunities.

A Gifted Child Dr. Grace LaJoy Henderson
IN FOSTER CARE

Recognize your power - Regardless of who you are or what you have been through, you have the power to positively affect individuals, your family, your community, and the world!

Be confident - Regardless of what anyone says, know that something good can come out of everything you experience in your life.

Take advantage of opportunities - If your parent, teacher, or employer asks you to do a task that seems difficult, take the challenge! Know that if they asked you to do it, they believe you are capable. If you begin to do it and get stuck, ask for help, but do not give up until you have completed the task.

Finally, remember these five things:
- You were born for a purpose.
- You have the ability to set and achieve goals.
- No one else can use your gifts and talents the way you can.
- Your adversity is a stepping-stone to take you to another level.
- Don't give up!

Empowerment for Children 81

A Gifted Child
IN FOSTER CARE

Dr. Grace LaJoy Henderson

A Gifted Child
IN FOSTER CARE

Dr. Grace LaJoy Henderson

14 – *Empowerment for Parents*

The word "gift" is defined as an unlearned talent. This means that a person who has a gift did not have to go to school to learn it. One who has a gift enjoys using it.

All children are "gifted" in one way or another. But, they need someone to recognize it, make them aware of it, and assist them in nurturing it. The following steps will help you empower your child to excel in what he or she enjoys doing, is naturally good at and is passionate about:

Pay attention to what your child enjoys doing. Watch what your child does while he/she is playing with toys, outside, or with friends. Listen to what your child says about the activities that he/she is involved in. These things will help you to see what your child's gift is.

Recognize what your child is naturally good at. Listen to the compliments you receive from other people. Family members, teachers, friends, and church members sometimes detect what your child is naturally good at before you do. So, listen to what they have to say about him or her. When your child receives the same compliment from several people who do not know each

A Gifted Child
IN FOSTER CARE

Dr. Grace LaJoy Henderson

other and who have not had communication with each other, this may be a sign of what your child's gift could be.

Never take away the thing your child is naturally good at as a punishment for misbehaving. The thing your child is naturally good at may be the thing that eventually keeps your child from getting involved in undesirable things. Therefore, never take it away from them. Do not pinpoint what your child is passionate about and take it away as a punishment. In fact, if your child is misbehaving, you may consider allowing your child to have more involvement in his/her passion. This may help detour him/her from the misbehavior.

Encourage your child to do what he/she enjoys and is naturally good at. Compliment your child, and let him or her know you approve of what they enjoy doing and you are excited about what they are doing. If possible, make opportunities for your child to use what they are naturally good at to help, inspire, or encourage someone else.

Empowerment for Parents   84

A Gifted Child
IN FOSTER CARE

Dr. Grace LaJoy Henderson

Provide opportunities for your child to participate in the thing he/she enjoys. Research your child's passion and arrange for him or her to take classes and lessons pertaining to the thing he/she enjoys doing. Also, provide opportunities for your child to be around other children who enjoy doing the same thing. Encourage, but do not *pressure*, him or her to participate in the opportunities you provide. This increases the likelihood your child's passion will always be enjoyable.

Don't worry about money. Never ever tell your child what they desire to do is not good enough, glamorous enough, or that they will never make any money doing what they enjoy. To remedy that situation, encourage your child to learn more than one skill so he/she will have options. But, never "take away", or speak negatively about the money-making potential of your child's natural talents and interests.

Know that you have the power to shape your child's life. You have the power to shape and mold your child into an influential person. Whether it is positive or negative, you *will* have an affect your child's future!

Empowerment for Parents   85

A Gifted Child
IN FOSTER CARE

Dr. Grace LaJoy Henderson

POEM - HE'S WORTH IT
Written by Grace LaJoy Henderson

Fond thoughts of the baby that you bore
from you he'd never part
But now your child has become defiant
And he's ripping out your heart

At times, in your disappointment
you wonder, "Did I birth this?"
When you observe his defiance
you wonder, "Is it worth this?"

Well, your cries have been heard
and today I'm here to say
That "Yes, your child is worth it"
even when he refuses to obey

He's worth every sacrifice
he's worth every tear
He's worth every worry
he's worth every fear

He's worth every heartache
headache and pain
He's worth it when you feel
that you're about to go insane

He's worth every day off work
to get him back in school
He's worth it when he loses control
and unable to keep his cool

He's worth every trip you make
to conferences with his teachers
He's worth the counseling sessions you have
with counselors, psychologists and preachers

Continued →

Poem – He's Worth It

A Gifted Child
IN FOSTER CARE

Dr. Grace LaJoy Henderson

He's worth the principal conferences
and disagreements with school staff
He's worth it when he must beware
of your anger, your tantrum, your wrath!

He's worth it all when you go through
unsurety, insecurity, and doubt
He's worth it when he has no clue
what respect is all about

He's worth the drug treatment
you may have to take him to
He's worth every dollar that you spend
although he may break you

Although your child has taken you
through misery and strife
His soul is very special
and so is his precious life

He is your special child
regardless of what he's done
So, as long as you do not give up
the enemy has not won

So, continue to fight for your child
'cause when the battles through
Your determination will prevail
although your child is in debt to you

But, just because your child owes you his life
doesn't mean he should be forced to repay
'Cause if we all got what <u>we</u> deserve
we'd all be dead today

Many children turn their lives around
and that's a blessing, it's not luck
But, even if your child never changes
don't *ever* let it be said, "You gave up"

Poem – He's Worth It

A Gifted Child
IN FOSTER CARE

Dr. Grace LaJoy Henderson

Discussion Topics

Chapter 1 – Left By Mother:

Agree/Disagree – Many children in foster care believe it is their fault that they can't be with their parents. Discuss why you agree or disagree. In your opinion, what makes a child blame themselves for their parent's mistakes?

Chapter 2 – Living with Daddy

Agree/Disagree – Foster and adoptive parents should tell foster children only positive things about their birth parents. Discuss why you agree or disagree.

Agree/Disagree – Birth fathers are capable of raising children alone on a permanent basis. Discuss why you agree or disagree.

Chapter 3 – Grandmother

Agree/Disagree – Things that are implanted in children's minds, positive or negative, can affect them throughout their entire lifetime. Discuss why you agree or disagree.

Agree/Disagree – Extended family is important for children in foster care. Discuss why you agree or disagree.

Chapter 4 – Left by Father

Agree/Disagree – Foster homes should not be used as long-term care for children in foster care. Discuss why you agree or disagree.

Discussion Topics Continued→

A Gifted Child
IN FOSTER CARE

Dr. Grace LaJoy Henderson

Agree/Disagree –Children who reside with only their father are more likely to be abandoned and end up in foster care than children who reside with only their mother. Discuss why you agree or disagree.

Discuss your thoughts and feelings about the children in the story being left in a home that eventually ended up with no food, lights, gas, water, or phone.

Chapter 5 – Living in Foster Care
Agree/Disagree – It is uncommon for children living in foster care to be labeled as gifted and talented. Discuss why you agree or disagree.

Agree/Disagree – Emergency foster care is necessary in many cases where children are removed from their home. Discuss why you agree or disagree.

Agree/Disagree – Many relatives of foster children give up after attempting to step in and care for them because they find the responsibility is greater than they expected. Discuss why you agree or disagree.

Agree/Disagree – Many children come into foster care with no belongings. Discuss why you agree or disagree.

Chapter 6 – Separated from Siblings
Agree/Disagree – Birth order plays a part in the way children are affected by abandonment. Discuss why you agree or disagree.

Discussion Topics Continued→

A Gifted Child
Dr. Grace LaJoy Henderson
IN FOSTER CARE

Agree/Disagree – Siblings who were born to the same parent(s) and lived in the same home can be affected in entirely different ways by the same event (good or bad). (I.e. one ends up going to college and one ends up using drugs for the rest of his/her life.) Discuss why you agree or disagree.

Agree/Disagree – If at all possible, siblings in foster care should be placed together in the same foster home. Discuss why you agree or disagree.

Agree/Disagree – Children in foster care who are separated from their siblings benefit from regular visits with them. Discuss why you disagree or disagree.

Chapter 7 – A Typical Day in Foster Care
Agree/Disagree – It is important for foster parents to delegate household chores to children in foster care. Discuss why you agree or disagree.

Chapter 8 – Life After Foster Care
Agree/Disagree – Foster care is dedicated to providing for the total well-being of children in foster care. Discuss some examples of how the foster care program provides for children in foster care.

Chapter 9 – Life After Foster Care
Agree/Disagree – Children who are released from foster care before they are legally an adult are likely to experience turmoil. Discuss why you agree or disagree.

Discussion Topics Continued→

A Gifted Child
IN FOSTER CARE   *Dr. Grace LaJoy Henderson*

Agree/Disagree – When children in foster care are moved often, it becomes difficult for them to make lasting friendships with other children. Discuss why you agree or disagree.

Chapter 10 – Daddy Left Again
Agree/Disagree – A foster child who is abandoned once and reunited, is at risk of being abandoned again. Discuss why you agree or disagree.

Agree/Disagree – Many children in foster care have gifts and talents that go unnoticed. Discuss why you agree or disagree.

Agree/Disagree – Switching schools is a big issue for children in foster care and every move can put them further behind in their education. Discuss why you agree or disagree. Please discuss some ways to keep children from falling behind as a result of switching homes and schools.

Agree/Disagree – It is common for children who have been abused or abandoned by their birth parent to still love them and want to reunite with them. Discuss why you agree or disagree.

Chapter 11 – Pregnant at Seventeen
Agree/Disagree – The likelihood of teenagers becoming unwed parents is greater when a child is in foster care. Discuss why you agree or disagree.

Discussion Topics Continued→

A Gifted Child   *Dr. Grace LaJoy Henderson*
IN FOSTER CARE

Agree/Disagree – Foster Care programs offer services to assist unwed teenage parents who are in foster care. Discuss why you agree or disagree.

Agree/Disagree – When a teenager becomes an unwed parent, it is likely that he/she will not be successful in life. Discuss why you agree or disagree. Discuss ways to help unwed teenage parents become successful.

Chapter 12 – My Gift Revealed

Agree/Disagree – The experiences children go through in their life are what shape them into the person who they eventually become. Discuss why you agree or disagree.

Chapter 13 – Empowerment for Children

Agree/Disagree – Every child is affected in some way by the choice(s) of someone else. Discuss why you agree or disagree.

Agree/Disagree – Children who have had negative life experiences will benefit from letting go of those disappointments, forgiving and moving on. Discuss why you agree or disagree.

Chapter 14 – Empowerment for Parents

Agree/Disagree – Every child is gifted in one way or the other. Discuss why you agree or disagree.

Agree/Disagree – Children need assistance from adults to recognize and begin to use their gifts and talents. Discuss why you agree or disagree.

A Gifted Child
IN FOSTER CARE

Dr. Grace LaJoy Henderson

Grace LaJoy's Life Timeline

November 1966
Grace LaJoy was
born in Grand
Rapids Michigan

1968
Grace's mother
left children with
father in KCMO

1972
Grace's first
experience with
poetry

1973
Grace's father
left children in
house alone

1973
Grace went to
emergency foster
care

1973
Grace lived in
two more foster
homes

1973
Grace lived with
Grandmother

1973
Grace lived in
Big Mama's
foster home

1975
Grace was placed
in Gifted and
Talented class

Summer 1976
Grace gets out
of foster care;
moves to NC

1976-1979
Daddy took
Grace from state
to state

Summer 1979
Daddy left again,
leaving Grace in
North Carolina

Summer 1979
Grace lived with
sister in North
Carolina

1980
Grace kept first
poem. Her sister
noticed her gift to
write

1980
Seventh Grade
teacher noticed
Grace's gift to
write

1981
Teacher noticed
Grace's creative
talent

Spring 1983
Sister moved to
Kansas City.
Older brother
moved into town
home

Summer 1983
Grace moved to
Kansas City to
live with older
sister again

Timeline continued→

93

A Gifted Child
IN FOSTER CARE

Dr. Grace LaJoy Henderson

Fall 1983
Grace began
senior year in
Kansas City

Fall 1983
Grace's father
lived with Grace
and her older
sister briefly

Fall 1983
Grace won
football
homecoming
queen

Fall 1983
Grace's poetry
placed in
school's contest

1983-1984
Several teachers
noticed Grace's
gift of writing

Spring 1984
Grace had written
70-80 poems

Summer 1984
Grace got
pregnant at
seventeen

January 1985
Grace began
living on her own

April 1985
Grace gave birth
to Arica

1986
Grace's Father
lived with her
and her baby
briefly in her
Kansas City
apartment

1987
Grace married
Arica's father

May 1988
Grace gave birth
to Aric

October 1988
Grace was
divorced

June 1992
Grace began
volunteering with
children at her
local church

1993
Grace realized
writing was her
gift

1994
Grace returned
to college

1995
Grace earned
Associate's
degree

1997
Grace earned
Bachelor's
degree

Timeline continued→

94

A Gifted Child
IN FOSTER CARE

Dr. Grace LaJoy Henderson

February 2004
Grace published
first book

May 2005
Grace earned
Doctorate degree

2005-2009
Grace published
twelve books
and three CDs

May 2006
Grace conducted
her first annual
Writer's
Breakthrough™
workshop for
writers and
aspiring authors

2007
Grace began
conducting
Sexual Purity
workshops and
classes for young
women

2009
Grace became a
professional
speaker and
workshop leader

2017
Grace published
The Gracie
Series of six
children's books

2018
Grace found her
mother after
forty-nine years!

2020
Grace published
the Finding
Mother series of
four books

2020
Grace revised
A Gifted Child in
Foster Care
and published
a Revised Edition

2009-2020
Grace has
published a total
of over thirty
books

A Gifted Child
IN FOSTER CARE   *Dr. Grace LaJoy Henderson*

Glossary of Terms

Assistance – Help received from an agency or other organization to help people who are in need.

Birth Order – The order in which siblings are born to their biological parents.

Brother – A male who is born by the same parents as someone else.

Case Worker – A person who works for the state who ensures that the needs of children and families in foster care are met according to specific state guidelines.

Child – A boy or girl between the age of zero and seventeen years old.

Educator – A person who teaches children in a school setting.

Empower – To give someone something that makes them able to do something that they were unable to do prior to receiving what you gave them.

Encourage – To offer someone something that causes them to begin or continue doing something positive.

Father – A male who participates in the making of child with a woman who gives birth to the child as a result of his participation.

A Gifted Child
IN FOSTER CARE
                                    Dr. Grace LaJoy Henderson

Foster Child – A child who becomes a ward of the state and lives in a foster home due to being unable to live with natural parents for one or more reasons.

Foster Parent – An adult who contracts with the foster care program to allow a child that is not their own to live in their home while taking care of all of the child's needs.

Gift – A natural unlearned talent that a person has.

Gifted Child – A child who has the ability to understand and apply what he/she learns faster than other children who are the same age and/or on the same grade level; A child who has an unlearned, natural talent to perform a task or do something that most children are unable to do; more advanced and focused than peers.

Grandmother – A female whose child becomes a mother or father.

Life Experience – An event or series of events or situations that occur during the course of a person's life.

Mother – A female who gives birth to a child.

Parent – A mother or father.

Permanency – a permanent place for a foster child to live. May be accomplished through the child being reunified with birth parents or adopted by a relative or other adoptive parent.

School – A place, usually a building, where students go to be taught by an educator or teacher.

A Gifted Child
IN FOSTER CARE   *Dr. Grace LaJoy Henderson*

Sibling – One who is, or who has, a brother or sister.

Sister – A female who is born by the same parents as someone else.

Social Service – Assistance from the state, or other agency or organization that helps families in need.

State Program – A program designed to assist families in need.

Teacher – One who educates children in a school setting.

Turbulent – Heavy movement; negative; turmoil.

Reunification – When a foster child and their parent or legal guardian are allowed to live together again as a family after foster care.

Separated – To be moved or taken away from another person or a familiar setting.

Visits – The time foster children spend with siblings, birth parents, or relatives while in foster care.

A Gifted Child   Dr. Grace LaJoy Henderson
IN FOSTER CARE

Index

Aric 72,94
Arica 69,70-72,94
Assistance 24,92,97,99
Big Mama 30-35,37,39-41,43-45,47-50,53,93
Birth Order 40,89,97
Brother 9-11,21,25-27,37-39,41,43,53,54,59, 67,
69,93,97,99
Carla 38,39,54,59,62,63,65,67
Case Worker 3,4,29,35,97
Child 1-4,7,8,10,11,17-21,23-25,30,34,46,55,59,64,
71-73,75-79,83-94,97-99
Daddy 15-19,24,25,31,35,50,53,54,57,59,64,65,72,
88,91,93
Danisha 37,39,43-46,54,59
Easter Mae 70
Educator 97,98
Emergency Foster Care 89,93
Empower 61,80,83,97
Encourage 84,85,97
Father 7-9,11,15,18,21,23-26,32,34,35,39,40,53-
57,59,63,67,70-72,78,88,89,93,94,97,98
Foster Care 1-4,29,32,35,37-41,43,49,50-52,57,
59,63,73,75,78-80,88-93,97-99
Foster Care Program 3,4,90,92,98
Foster Child(ren) 1,2,34,78,88,89,91,97-99
Foster Parent(s) 2,49,90,98
Gift(s) 38,61,62,74-77,80,81,83,84,91,92,94,98
Gifted 1,2,4,5,33,34,37,49,50,63,74,78,80,83,89,
92,93,98
Gifted and Talented Program 3,4,33,34,78

99

Gracie 7,10,21,38
Grandmother 7,18-25,30,31,39,50,53,88,93,98
Grayson 37-39,67
Jerome 15,39-41,67,69
Life Experience 1,80,92,98
Mother 1,7-13,15,19,23,35,40,41,61,69,70,73,77-79,88,89,93,98
Nena 76,77
Papa 32,41,43,44,47-49
Parent 3,4,69,75,81,88,90-92,98,99
Peaches 71
Permanency 4,98
Reunification 99
School 4,8,9,21,23,24,26,27,33,34,37,44-50,54, 55, 57,59,63,64,67,68,76,83,86,87,94,97-99
Separated 2,3,37,40,41,89,99
Sibling 7,9,10,15-17,21,34,37,39-41,53,55,89,90, 97,99
Sister 9-11,19,21,26,27,30,35,37-39,41,43,46,53, 54,59,67,69-71,93,94,98
Social Service 2,3,30,31,99
State Program 3,99
Teacher 23,24,27,33,34,46,62,63,68,76,81,83,86, 93,94,98,99
Terrance 37-39
Turbulent 1,8,99
Visits 34,35,37,39,40,90,99

A Gifted Child
IN FOSTER CARE

Dr. Grace LaJoy Henderson

FINDING MOTHER SERIES

When Grace LaJoy originally published her foster care story, *A Gifted Child in Foster Care*, she thought she would *never* find her mother. But, she found her after 49 years! Now she is sharing her fascinating journey in an inspiring series you will love!

Titles include:
Finding Mother After Five Decades: *A Story of Hope*
Reuniting with Mother: *A Story of Tenacity*
After the Reunion: *A Story of Acceptance*
Diary of Emotions: *Thoughts and Feelings*

Discussion Questions in the back of each book are designed to increase awareness and discussion about mental health. **Questions Teachers Can Ask** aid in increasing reading comprehension skills in the classroom.

This inspiring series offers hope to anyone searching for a lost loved one. You enjoyed Grace LaJoy's foster care story. Now, collect the entire Finding Mother Series today!

Available in softcover and Kindle eBook
Collect them all at Amazon.com
www.gracelajoy.com

A Gifted Child
IN FOSTER CARE

Dr. Grace LaJoy Henderson

Finding Mother After Five Decades: A Story of Hope

Grace LaJoy's determination pays off when she finally finds her mother who abandoned her at age two. Discover the specific details of her intriguing journey in *Finding Mother after Five Decades*, BOOK 1 of the Finding Mother Series

Reuniting with Mother: A Story of Tenacity

What happens when Grace LaJoy and her siblings come face-to-face with their estranged mother after 49 years? How does she receive them? Find out in *Reuniting with Mother*, BOOK 2 of the Finding Mother Series

After the Reunion: A Story of Acceptance

After a very emotional reunion, Grace LaJoy has two concerns to address with her long-lost mother. What are her concerns? Does she get the answers she needs from her mother? Find out in *After the Reunion*, BOOK 3 of the Finding Mother Series

Diary of Emotion: Thoughts and Feelings

After reuniting with her mother after 49 years, Grace LaJoy toils with an array of thoughts and feeling. She reveals them all in *Diary of Emotions*, BOOK 4 of the Finding Mother Series

www.ingramcontent.com/pod-product-compliance
Lightning Source LLC
Chambersburg PA
CBHW052101070526
44584CB00017B/2278